OWNING A SELF-PUBLISHING COMPANY FOR YOUR BOOK(S)

Table of Contents

Here are the steps to help you on your journey..3

Module 1..3

   Acquiring Company L.L.C. & Tax I.D #...3

   Lesson 1: Tax I.D 6

Module 2..7

   Create Logo and own your Logo..7

   Lesson 1: Own Your Logo..8

   Lesson 2: Trademark your logo to protect it from being stolen...................................8

   Lesson 3: Copyright vs. Trademark...9

   Lesson 4: The difference between copyright and trademark.......................................9

   Lesson 5: Copyright Protection...9

   Lesson 6: How copyright works...10

   Lesson 7: Trademark Protection..11

   Lesson 8: How to Copyright a Logo 12

   Lesson 9: How to Trademark a Logo...13

   Lesson 10: How to trademark a logo design..14

Writing your book without a publishing business...14

Module 3..15

   Title Your Book..15

   Lesson 1: Things to Consider When Titling a Book..16

   Lesson 2: Tips for Coming Up With the Best Book Title...17

Module 4..18

   Write book & Create cover 18

Module 5..18

   Find self publishing company & Print on demand (P.O.D)...18

   Lesson 1: Acquire International Standard Book Number (ISBN).................................19

Module 6..21

   Publish your book & book cover..21

THE MATCH OF LIFE!

Module 1

Acquiring Company L.L.C. & Tax I.D

Acquiring L.L.C. & Tax I.D # is what's needed to start any legal business. It's not as hard as you may think. To acquire a L.L.C. You must first have the name of your company. After you have a company name. You must log into your [state licensing website](#), in most states it's the Secretary of state. The best way and easiest is just go to Google search and type the state you live in then put LLC behind the name. I live in Michigan; this is how to fill out a L.L.C for Michigan. Other state forms will be worded different but are still pretty must the same in each state. I've filled in the blanks for a better understanding...

MICHIGAN DEPARTMENT OF LICENSING AND REGULATORY AFFAIRS
CORPORATIONS, SECURITIES & COMMERCIAL LICENSING BUREAU

Date Received	AC1	(FOR BUREAU USE ONLY)
	This document is effective on the date filed, unless a subsequent effective date within 90 days after received date is stated in the document.	

Name
Owner of the company L.L.C.

Address
This form will be returned to this address

City	State	ZIP Code

EFFECTIVE DATE:

Document will be returned to the name and address you enter above.
If left blank, document will be returned to the registered office.

ARTICLES OF ORGANIZATION
For use by Domestic Limited Liability Companies
(Please read information and instructions on reverse side)

Pursuant to the provisions of Act 23, Public Acts of 1993, the undersigned executes the following Articles:

ARTICLE I

The name of the limited liability company is: Name of the company with the letters L.L.C after the company name.

ARTICLE II

The purpose or purposes for which the limited liability company is formed is to engage in any activity within the purposes for which a limited liability company may be formed under the Limited Liability Company Act of Michigan.
State everything that the company doing under the company L.L.C.

ARTICLE III

The duration of the limited liability company if other than perpetual is: Leave blank

ARTICLE IV

1. The name of the resident agent at the registered office is: Owner of the Company

2. The street address of the location of the registered office is:

This address is usually the same as the mailing address at the top of this document , Michigan _____
(Street Address)   (City)   (Zip Code)

3. The mailing address of the registered office if different than above:

_____ , Michigan _____
(P.O. Box or Street Address)   (City)   (Zip Code)

ARTICLE V (Insert any desired additional provision authorized by the Act; attach additional pages if needed.)

Usually leave blank.

Signed this_____Day_____ day of _____Month_____ , _____Year_____

By_____
(Signature(s) of Organizer(s))

The Owners of the company Sign above Print below

Preparer's Name <u>Usually the Owner</u>

Business telephone number (_____) <u>Your contact number</u>

INFORMATION AND INSTRUCTIONS

1. This form may be used to draft your Articles of Organization. A document required or permitted to be filed under the act cannot be filed unless it contains the minimum information required by the Act. The format provided contains only the minimal information required to make the document fileable and may not meet your needs. This is a legal document and agency staff cannot provide legal advice.

2. Submit one original of this document. Upon filing, the document will be added to the records of the Corporations, Securities & Commercial Licensing Bureau. The original will be returned to your registered office address unless you enter a different address in the box on the front of this document.
   Since this document will be maintained on electronic format, it is important that the filing be legible. Documents with poor black and white contrast, or otherwise illegible, will be rejected.

3. This document is to be used pursuant to the provisions of Act 23, P.A. of 1993, by one or more persons for the purpose of forming a domestic limited liability company. **Use form BCS/CD 701 if the limited liability company will be providing services rendered by a dentist, an osteopathic physician, a physician, a surgeon, a doctor of divinity or other clergy, or an attorney-at-law.**

4. Article I - The name of a domestic limited liability company is required to contain the words Limited Liability Company or the abbreviation L.L.C. or L.C., with or without periods.

5. Article II- Under section 203(b) of the Act, it is sufficient to state substantially, alone or with specifically enumerated purposes, that the limited liability company is formed to engage in any activity within the purposes for which a limited liability company may be formed under the Act.

6. Article V - Section 401 of the Act specifically states the business shall be managed by members unless the Articles of Organization state the business will be managed by managers. If the limited liability company is to be managed by managers instead of by members, insert a statement to that effect in Article V.

7. This document is effective on the date endorsed "Filed" by the Bureau. A later effective date, no more than 90 days after the date of delivery, may be stated as an additional article.

8. The Articles must be signed by one or more persons organizing the Limited Liability Company. Type or print the name of the organizers signing beneath their signature.

9. If more space is needed, attach additional pages. All pages should be numbered.

10. **NONREFUNDABLE FEE:** Make remittance payable to the State of Michigan. Include limited liability company name on check or money order...**$50.00**
    Veterans: Pursuant to MCL 450.5101(7)(8)(10), if a majority of the initial membership interests in the domestic limited liability company will be held by 1 or more veterans who served in the United States Armed Forces, (including the reserve components) who were discharged or released under conditions other than dishonorable, you may obtain further information regarding a fee waiver at www.michigan.gov/corpveteranfeewaivers.

Submit with check or money order by mail:
Michigan Department of Licensing and Regulatory Affairs
Corporations, Securities & Commercial Licensing Bureau
Corporations Division
P.O. Box 30054
Lansing, MI 48909

To submit in person:
2407 N Grand River Ave
Lansing, MI 48906
Telephone: (517) 241-6470
Fees may be paid by check, money order, VISA, MasterCard, American Express, or Discover.

COFS (Corporations Online Filing System):
This document may be completed and submitted online at www.michigan.gov/corpfileonline
Fees may be paid by VISA, MasterCard, American Express, or Discover.

Documents that are endorsed filed are available at www.michigan.gov/corpentitysearch. If the submitted document is not fileable, the notice of refusal to file and document will be available at the Rejected Filings Search website at www. michigan.gov/corprejectedsearch.

LARA is an equal opportunity employer/program. Auxiliary aids, services and other reasonable accommodations are available upon request to individuals with disabilities.

Lesson 1: Tax I.D

1. Log into irs.gov

2. in the search bar type: tax I.D #

3. Scroll down click on EMPLOYER IDENTIFICATION NUMBER

4. Click on EIN-online

5. Read all 3 steps

6. Click on: Apply Online Now

7. Read everything then click continue

8. Scroll down to limited liability company (LLC). Click the dot next to it (LLC) then click continues.

9. Read what a limited liability company is. Then scroll down and click continue.

10. Put 1 in the box that asks how many members are in the LLC? Which are you?

11. Then pick the state where the L.L.C will operate from. Then click continue.

12. Read the page on single-member limited liability Company then click continues.

13. Click the dot. Saying started a new business, click continues.

14. Fill-in first and last name along with social security number (The IRS wants you do to be a taxpayer in order to receive an EIN). Click in the dot saying I am one owner, members or the managing member of this LLC. Then click continue.

15. Fill in the address where the LLC will be operating from. Fill in the info from your Articles of Organization, then click continue.

16. Fill in all the dots which all should be NO. Since you're just starting out.

17. Scroll down to other, click the dot. Then click continue.

18. Scroll down again to other. In the box write: Book Publishing.

Finally. In order to receive your EIN confirmation letter. There are 2 ways to receive it. Which is online or by mail.

1. If you choose to receive it online. Click the circle next to online. Then click continue. Then it can be printed out on your printer.

2. To receive it by mail which may take up to 4 weeks to receive your EIN confirmation letter just click to receive by mail and follow the steps.

Getting a EIN from the IRS is **Free.** In case you didn't know, unless you have someone do the work for you.

Module 2

Create Logo and own your Logo

If you have an ideal for a logo for your company. And can describe your ideal plus do some kind of drawing for your logo. Here is some companies, that can bring your logo to life.

- ❖ primelogostudio.com
- ❖ logoaspire.com
- ❖ thelogosquad.com
- ❖ logoorbit.com
- ❖ staples.com/logo/directory logo
- ❖ logoconcave.com
- ❖ tailoredlogo.com
- ❖ officedepot.com
- ❖ logoperfecto.com
- ❖ brandcrowd.com

I personally use fiverr (fiverr.com) for my logo and other digital need. I've always been very happy with fiverr.

THE MATCH OF LIFE..

This Logo was created by fiverr.com

Lesson 1: Own Your Logo

Your brand name was chosen, your [logo was designed](#) and the [logo files were delivered](#)—now you need to protect your brand assets.

There are many unscrupulous people out there ready to infringe on your creative intellectual property.

Lesson 2: Trademark your logo to protect it from being stolen.

No matter the size or the industry your company operates in, you should [file for logo trademark](#) yourself or [hire a trademark attorney](#) **which can cost you a lot** to do it for you.

When you hear property attorneys describe the difference of both: copyright and trademark laws.

❖   Copyright covers creative works of expression fixed into a tangible medium of expression.

❖   Trademark covers business names, slogans and other items used to identify it in the marketplace.

However, there is a great deal of overlap between two areas of copyright and trademark, and businesses are known for using both to protect their logos from undesired use.

❖   Copyright is designed to protect against almost all unlicensed copying that is outside of fair use.

❖   Trademark only deals with use of the mark that causes confusion in that company's marketplace.

In short, trademark is designed not to prevent copying, but confusion in the marketplace, thus severely limiting what uses of the logo can be considered infringing.

Lesson 3: Copyright vs. Trademark

The only way to achieve protection is through a copyright, trademark or both. And here lies the confusion with logos - many of them actually qualify for both trademark and copyright protection.

Lesson 4: The difference between copyright and trademark

In order to have a better understanding of how copyright and trademark work, it's helpful to know which type of intellectual properties each one protects.

The biggest difference between them is that copyrighting won't protect your brand's name and logo from infringement, but a trademark will.

1. Copyright is made for artistic works protection (i.e. its authorship)

A common symbol for the copyright is ©, but you can also add 'Copyright' or 'Copr.' and even your name and year the work was published. For example "© 2018 by ebaqdesign" at the bottom of my website claims right to everything on it.

2. Trademark is made to prevent confusion in the company's marketplace.

There are different symbols for trademark protection:

* ™ for the unregistered trademark

* SM for the unregistered service trademark

* ® for the registered trademark

The process of both copyright and trademark takes time to get final approval, but by starting now you preserve your rights to ownership and thus legal remedy. On the other hand, if you don't have a trademark or copyright you may not be able to sue another party for infringement of your logo.

Lesson 5: Copyright Protection

You already have a copyright in your logo at the moment you draw it?

Did you know that due to The U.S. Copyright Law, every original work of authorship is under protection, automatically?

On its most basic level, copyright of unique visual design is automatic, and originates with the designer.

Any unique logo that I designed for a client will have automatically had copyright assigned to it, and to me.

Read more about copyright basics for graphic designers on AIGA's website.

The copyright law protects "original works of authorship" expressed in a physical form (i.e. books, movies, songs, paintings, photos, choreography, logos etc.)

However, copyright does not protect facts, ideas, systems, or methods of operation, it protects the only the unique way you expressed these things in your work.

In other words, copyright law protects the "expression" of an idea, but copyright does not protect the "idea" itself.

The distinction between the idea and the expression is fundamental in the Copyright law.

Read more about it in **Copyright Act of 1976**.

Lesson 6: How copyright works

Copyright law grants authors and artists the exclusive right to make and sell copies of their works, the right to create derivative works, and the right to perform or display their works publicly.

In order for a work to have copyright protection, it must reach a requisite level of creativity.

Many logos, however, do not - this is one difficulty about logo copyright registration.

Since copyright can't protect a name, colors or the design of the logo, most simple logos simply do not have the required level of creativity to be considered copyrightable.

When you register the copyright, you are able to sue everybody, who tries to copy your work or exploit it for his own purposes.

Since your copyright is registered federally, you are in charge of your property usage, publishing, distribution, and presentation to the audience.

That's why you must transfer the copyright to the client at the time of the logo artwork delivery.

Lesson 7: Trademark Protection

Trademark is about protecting things that identify a business in the marketplace and logos are among the most important means of identification.

As such, logos are generally protected by trademark and enforceable as such.

Trademark protects all details of your work (names, words, colors, font etc.)

Trademark can be words combination, symbol or type of design, which differentiate your particular brand from many others, who are offering same products and services, as you.

While copyright protects your work authorship, a trademark protects all the details so no one else can use it.

Trademark protects details like: mark, name, font, colors.

If you want to protect your brand identity you have to **register a trademark** for your company name, logos, and slogans.

By using the trademark symbol, you notify other people that products they use are your property.

In order to prevent unauthorized use of your mark by third parties, you have to choose a strong one.

Brands, which are **the most powerful** nowadays, are the excellent example of how strong mark should be created.

Looking at the brands such as Google, Apple or Microsoft we can see examples of how to create a strong trademark:

> ❖ Registering the name, which doesn't exist as the word; a simple word, which is totally unrelated to the products you produce; words, which are generic to your product (f.e. 'Cookies' for a specific type of cookies) either obviously describe things you produce (f.e. 'Peanut bar' for the bar with the peanut).

The three symbols that represent trademark are the circled R (®), little capital letters TM (™), and the little capital letters SM (℠).

Trademark symbols: R, TM, SM

The circled R can only be used once you have a federal registration.

This means you've applied for it and received a trademark registration from the US government.

This is serious, because using that circled R is actually a violation of federal law unless you have the trademark, even when application is pending.

However, you can use the (™) from the moment you apply, or before.

For example:

❖ You're a lawyer that offers legal services. It's a service mark (SM).

❖ You sell goods, e.g. clothing. It's a trademark (™).

Have some questions about the trademark law what remain unanswered?

Check this **Trademark FAQ**.

Lesson 8: How to Copyright a Logo

I assume that your home country is US.

If you're looking to for specific instructions on how to do the process in the UK check **this article instead.**

Before **claiming the copyright**, do a research among all existing logos on the U.S. Copyright Office website to ensure your logo design is unique.

Besides, it is crucial to officially define, who holds the copyright for the logo (the creator of logo or business, for which this logo was made) to prevent possible conflicts about further actions.

How much does it cost to copyright a logo? It can cost you anywhere from $35-85 depending if you apply online or by mail, and if you select the category (less work for USCO).

How to copyright a logo step-by-step:

- ❖ Fill out the <u>application online</u> on the official site of United States Copyright Office. Besides, you can also submit the application in a paper form.

- ❖ Pay a registration fee (for the logo it's $39) with a card, electronic check or your deposit account with the U.S. Copyright Office.

- ❖ Send nonreturnable copies of your logo (if it was already published somewhere you have to send two copies if it wasn't yet – only one).

- ❖ Wait for a confirmation mail.

Despite the way you apply for the copyright and the application phase, your copyright is effective since the date you submitted the form, NOT the date of its approval.

As for registered copyright, you can protect usage of your logo, its publishing, distribution, and control how it is presented to the public.

Lesson 9: How to Trademark a Logo

Having a registered trademark helps your clients to differentiate products from services your brand offers.

But before you start you trademarking process:

Make sure that your logo is available for your adoption and use.

Lesson 10: How to trademark a logo design

As well as for the copyright, you should search <u>the USPTO's database</u> for trademarks, similar to your logo, and evaluate ones you find for possible conflicts.

It will save you both money and efforts you could spend for the whole registration procedure because the USPTO doesn't make any research for similar logos until the very moment you submit the application.

For registering a trademark for your logo you have to:

❖ File an application via **Trademark Electronic Application System** (TEAS), which requires a detailed description of your logo and what it represents.

❖ Check the status of your application (normally it takes about 4 months to finish the process, but it may vary).

❖ Set up a "trademark watch" service to protect your rights.

In case of registered trademark, you can protect your brand identity and, what is the most important – prevent usage of your name and design by third parties.

Writing your book without a publishing business

Module 3

Title Your Book

A good title will generate interest and intrigue readers without giving away too much plot. Titles may seem secondary to story but the perfect book title can make a novel or nonfiction book that much more memorable in the minds of readers while turning your work into a bestseller.

Good titles have certain traits in common. It can be useful to write down a list of titles of some of your favorite books and think about what makes them work as titles. Some of the characteristics that good titles share are:

* **Short**. The most memorable titles are usually on the shorter side. A short title is easy to remember and oftentimes can be more evocative and powerful than longer potential titles.

* **Evocative**. Best-selling titles are often evocative and contain compelling wordplay and imagery. Novel titles are a small showcase of your abilities as a writer. As such, it's important to come up with a great title that will show potential readers a bit of your writing skills.

* **Memorable and unique**. A good-book-title should be both memorable and unique. The perfect is easily identifiable and unforgettable.

Lesson 1: Things to Consider When Titling a Book

One word titles. Many best-selling titles are only one word but in the age of online search engines it's important to consider the consequences of choosing a one word title. When typing a one word title into a search engine, a potential reader will pull up a list with many results outside of your book. Consider expanding one word titles to three -word titles or even four-words to make search results more specific to your book.

* **Existing titles**. It's important to make sure that you are choosing an original title that hasn't already been used by an existing book. Make sure to extensively search the working title of a new book on search engines to ensure that it hasn't already been used.

* **Consider genre**. Think about what genre you're working within and come up with the right title accordingly. Convention dictates that a thriller will have a different sort of title than a fantasy novel. Your book's title should be similar to other book titles within the same genre so readers have some idea what sort of story your book contains.

* **Inadvertent references**. An important factor to consider when titling your book, is making sure that the title of your book doesn't inadvertently reference any controversial topics. Successful book marketing requires a great book title that won't make readers associate the title of the book with a controversial topic or group.

Lesson 2: Tips for Coming Up With the Best Book Title

It can be tough to arrive at the right title for your book. Here are some things you might want to consider when generating ideas for a new title for your book:

* **Character Names**. Consider naming your book after your main character or another important character in your book. Are there characters in our book with unique or evocative names? Character names, like *Harry Potter*, can provide strong and simple novel titles that grab a potential reader's attention.

* **Setting**. Think about where and when your book is set. Playing on the setting in your story title can help generate possible titles that would interest readers. *Love in the Time of Cholera* is a well known book title that immediately establishes time period and tone.

* **Literary Devices**. Many attention-grabbing non-fiction titles and fiction titles use literary devices to spice up their titles. You might consider using alliteration, like *Gone Girl*, or double entendre to produce a catchy title that hooks a reader's interest.

* **Originality**. Consider what separates your book from other books and try to incorporate it into your title ideas. The perfect title should clue the reader into

what makes your book special and separates it from others. *The Secret*, for example, is an intriguing book title that promises a wholly original literary experience.

Module 4

Write book & Create cover

This is the easy part. You already know what your book is about; it's time to put it on paper so to speak. The best way to write your book is used a talk-to-text on your computer. I use the site dictation.io it is very easy to use, I just love it. When I wanna check on my punctuation, I use <u>spellboy.com</u> these sites are very easy to use and free. If you want more in-depth help, you can use grammarly.com, you can also get free help from this site but you can use their paid help which I didn't ever. Remember, you wanna spend less as possible. Just cut and paste for all 3 sites just say what you feel what you want to write about go back edited the way you want to write it the way you want it to sound is just say as much as possible just Ramble On and talk about what your book is about what's in each chapter and then edit it later or have someone else write the book for you at a price which is known as a ghostwriter there are many Ghost Riders out there you could tell them what you want your book to be about and have them write the book or you can have them add to what you wrote in your book the thing is just Wright and just keep going and edited later as for the cover of your book there are many ways to get your cover done you can freelance it out and tell the person what you want done or you can draw yourself uploaded it to have the cover made the best company for all this for Ghost Rider and cover design I found Fiverr I've use others help me design and do other things but fiber comes out on top for me.

Module 5

Find self publishing company & Print on demand (P.O.D)

The most famous print-on-demand publishing companies include [BookBaby](), [Blurb](), and [IngramSpark](). You can check their websites for pricing details, but you can be sure to have your books seen on key distributors such as Barnes and Noble, Amazon, Apple Books, and Kobo. They also provide other services too, such as [book cover design](),[book editing](), and [formatting](). I personally use [ingramspark.com](). I love this company. They have my books in 40.000 distributors and libraries worldwide. I've had many sales by using ingramspark.

The P.O.D service will most likely get your book on their own bookstore as well. However, if you do plan to consider them, you would have to know what makes their print-on-demand services stand out from traditional publishing.
P.O.D may not be for every self-publishing author but is ideal for those who have seen some success with the proof of sales earlier in their books. This is primarily because of the discoverability they receive with POD services.

Lesson 1: Acquire International Standard Book Number (ISBN)

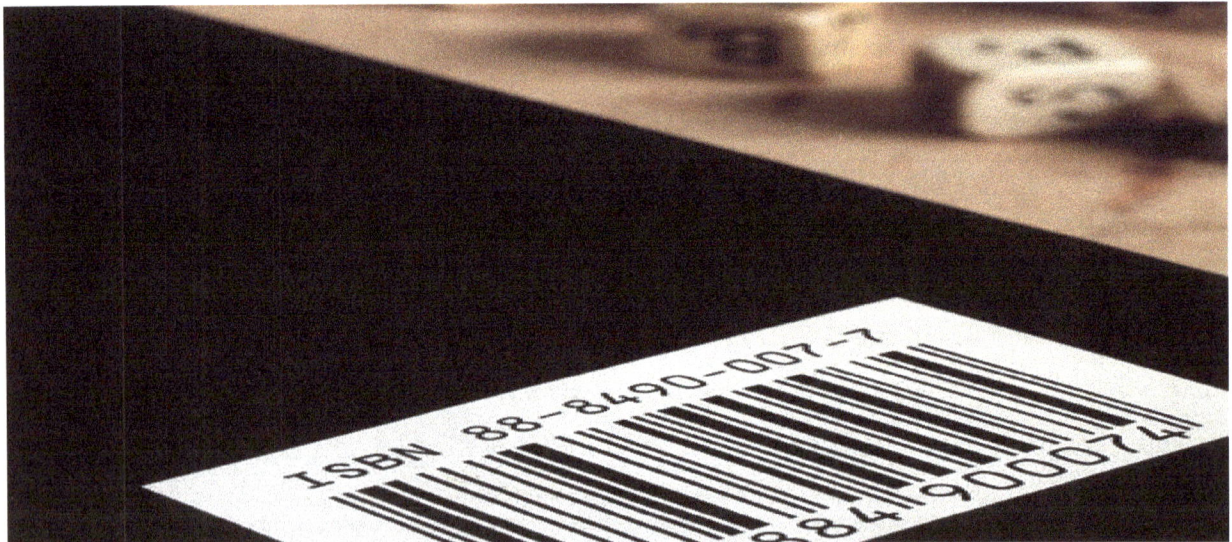

There are many reasons to purchase an ISBN for your title, including:

- ❖ An ISBN improves the likelihood your book will be found and purchased
- ❖ An ISBN links to essential information about your book
- ❖ An ISBN enables more efficient marketing and distribution of your title
- ❖ Most retailers require ISBNs
- ❖ Correct use of the ISBN allows different product forms and editions of a book, printed or digital, to be differentiated clearly, ensuring that customers receive the version they require
- ❖ An ISBN helps you collect and analyze book sales data
- ❖ An ISBN ensures your book's information will be stored in the *Books In Print* database
- ❖ *Books In Print* is consulted by publishers, retailers and libraries around world when searching for title information
- ❖ The ISBN conveys no legal or copyright protection, however, the use of ISBNs for publications is prescribed by law in some countries
- ❖ In some countries a book will be charged higher tax if it does not have an ISBN
- ❖ ISBNs are the global standard for book identification

  You will need one ISBN for each edition and format of your book. The ISBN identifies the publisher as well as the specific book title, edition and format (hardback, paperback, ePub, PDF, Mobi, Audio...). Any variation of a book would require the use of a unique ISBN to identify it properly. This allows retailers to help the customer understand exactly which version of a title they are purchasing. So, you should consider:

- ❖ How many book titles you are planning to publish
- ❖ How many formats will each title be created in
- ❖ Do you plan to publish future revised editions of these titles

  And remember:

- ❖ You can purchase ISBN's in advance and register your titles any time after they are obtained.
- ❖ ISBN's *never* expire.

Bowker(www.myidentifiers.com) is the official ISBN Agency for publishers physically located in the United States and its territories (Puerto Rico, Guam, US Virgin Islands, Northern Mariana Islands, American Samoa, as well as military bases and embassies. If an ISBN is obtained from a source other than the official ISBN Agency, it might not identify the publisher of the title accurately. This can have implications for doing business in the publishing industry supply chain.

Once you set up your account, your ISBN will be added to your account immediately at purchase (Title Assignment Instructions). You will be recognized as the publisher of all book titles associated with those ISBNs. For more information about the ISBN standard, or if you are looking for the official ISBN Agency in your jurisdiction, visit the International ISBN Agency.

Module 6

Publish your book & book cover

Once you create your manuscript file and book cover file. Now it's time to publish your book. It's not hard as it my sound. KDP (Amazon) is probably the most popular one, when I first started out on my self-publishing journey I used KDP I'll just say I didn't have a very good experience with KDP. But like I said before I discovered ingramspark and for me they were a lot better than KDP. The only problem with ingramspark is their customer service, it's terrible but everything else is great as far as getting your book out there on both book and ebook platforms. Remember you can use these other companies also:

BookBaby,

Blurb,

Promote book(s) on Facebook,Twitter,Instagram,Youtube etc.

 Create website for your book and apparel.

Create sayings from your book(s). To be placed on shirts etc.

Create books that will relate to your 1st and main book.

NOW YOU KNOW WHAT IT TAKES TO BE A SELF-PUBLISHING AUTHOR. PLUS HOW TO START A SELF-PUBLISHING COMPANY. OR ANY COMPANY. GO OUT AN CHANGE THE WORLD.....

www.ingramcontent.com/pod-product-compliance
Lightning Source LLC
Chambersburg PA
CBHW080603030426
42336CB00019B/3310